Katy Bowser Hutson,
Flo Paris Oakes, *and*
Tish Harrison Warren

Little Prayers
for
Ordinary Days

Illustrated by Liita Forsyth

ivp
Kids

K. B. H.
*Story and Del, for you
God made the world.*

F. P. O.
*For Sera and Amelie,
who display God's
limitless love, and
for Layla, may God
be with you always.*

T. H. W.
*To Raine, Flannery,
and Gus,
my very favorites.*

L. F.
*For all my students
at The Field
School Chicago.*

InterVarsity Press • P.O. Box 1400, Downers Grove, IL 60515-1426
ivpress.com • email@ivpress.com

Text ©2022 by Lutitia Harrison Warren, Florence Renee Oakes,
and Katherine J. Hutson

Illustrations ©2022 by InterVarsity Press, LLC

InterVarsity Press® is the book-publishing division of InterVarsity
Christian Fellowship/USA®, a movement of students and faculty
active on campus at hundreds of universities, colleges, and schools of
nursing in the United States of America, and a member movement of
the International Fellowship of Evangelical Students. For information
about local and regional activities, visit intervarsity.org.

Cover and interior illustrations: Liita Forsyth

ISBN 978-1-5140-0339-8 (print)
ISBN 978-1-5140-0340-4 (digital)
ISBN 978-1-5140-0549-1 (enhanced digital)

Printed in China

Library of Congress Cataloging-in-Publication Data

A catalog record for this book is available from the Library of Congress.

P	16	15	14	13	12	11	10	9	8	7	6	5	4	3	2	1
Y	35	34	33	32	31	30	29	28	27	26	25	24	23	22			

Sometimes it's easy to talk to God. Sometimes it feels hard. No matter how you feel, we made this book to help you.

Maybe these prayers will give you words for something you've been trying to say. Maybe you'll end up praying something that you'd never think about on your own.

You can pray these alone or with other people. Silently or out loud.

These prayers are for ordinary days. For playing, for school, for when you have big thoughts or little ones. God meets you in each moment.

You don't have to talk to God with big words or only about extra-special things. There is nothing that you're not allowed to say to God.

God always listens. God always loves you.

You can tell God everything.

For waking up

Dear God who made the morning,
Every day, you tell the sun to wake up.
Every day, you come close to us.
Again and again, you love us.
Thank you for this new day.

For looking in a mirror

God who made me, thank you for forming my body.
When I look in the mirror, I see your greatest creation.
You made me in your image.
You love how you made me.
I love how you made me too.

For the start of a school day

Dear God,

Bless our school

and our teachers

and all of our helpers.

Give me courage to be a good friend,

especially to those who don't yet have a friend.

It is a gift to learn new things about your world.

Let me be curious and kind.

And please keep everyone safe

all day long.

For the end of a school day

God, the time for school is done.

Thank you for each thing I learned.

Thank you that you were with me in each struggle.

Let me hold on to every

good,

true,

and beautiful thing

you showed me.

Now it's time to play and relax.

Yippee!

For reading a book

God the Storyteller, I love books!
The smell and feel of paper,
the pictures, and all of the words:
delightful words, hard words, interesting words!
What will happen when I turn the page?
You love stories too, God.
You are telling the biggest, best story with your world.
And I get to be in it—wow!

For listening to music

Dear God who sings over the world,
Thank you for music.
It helps me when I do my chores.
I like to listen to my favorite songs in the car.
I sing along and it feels so good—
and I know you like to hear it!

For making something

God, I love to make things!
When I paint, when I draw, when I write,
when I build, when I dance, when I cook, when I dig,
I am acting like you!
You love to make good things.
You do it all the time, and you never get tired.
I love that you made me a maker like you—
it gives you joy when I create.
I think you're amazing.

For trying something new

God, I am trying something new.

It's scary.

And exciting!

What if I don't get it right?

I know that I can't do anything

to make you love me more

or less.

You just love me

because you love me.

You are always with me,

cheering me on.

That gives me courage to try with all my heart.

For rest time

Dear God who rested after creating all of the earth,
You tell us that rest time is special.
A time to slow down.
A time to come close to you.
A time to hear what you might have to say to us.
Take my scary thoughts,
my heavy worries,
my tired body,
and give me rest.

For waiting

God, it is so hard to wait!
I have to wait my turn.
I have to wait on other people.
I have to wait for things I want.
It feels like it's taking forever!
While I wait, please wait with me.

For when I break something

God, I broke something.
I can't do anything to fix it.
I feel terrible and sad.
Please help me have courage to tell the truth.
Please help me say I'm sorry.
Thank you for caring about me
more than anything I break,
and for forgiving me—
over and over.

For when I have lost something

Dear God, I have lost something.

I really want to find it!

I feel frustrated and upset.

Will you help me find what I've lost?

Thank you that you love me so much

that you always

—always, always, always—

come after me to find me.

For seeing a friend

Dear God, I am so grateful that I can see my friend!
Thank you for making friendship and for making my friend.
Help me to love my friends, listen to them, and care for them.
You call me your friend.
Thank you that you are the very best friend!

For leaving a friend

Dear God, I am sad to leave my friend.
The time together went by so fast!
Please help my heart when the fun is over
and friends have to leave.
Help me to know you are still with me.

For doing chores

Dear God,
Sometimes it's hard to do work.
But I ask for the strength
to do my chores well.
Jesus worked—
to create,
to build,
to love,
and to heal.
Help me find some small joy
in my work today.

For when I do what I shouldn't

I don't know why,

but today

I keep doing things

that I know I shouldn't do.

I keep getting in trouble.

It is so hard to stop.

God, I need help.

You know it can be hard to do the right thing.

Please come close and whisper your love to me.

For being outside

Dear God who made the world,
The sunshine feels good on my skin.
The grass is tickly under my feet.
The breeze blows through the trees.
Sometimes the mosquitoes come
and I swat them away with my hand.
Sometimes a siren sounds loud on my street.
But I take a deep breath,
and I know you are here
among the people and the things
you have made.

For play time

Playful God,
Play is a gift you've given all of your creation.
Puppies wrestle, dolphins jump and dive,
and deer leap and romp.
Give me joy and laughter today as I play.

For petting an animal

Dear God who made all things,
I love this creature you made.
I pet her soft fur.
I tell her she is good.
Sometimes she licks my hand or
my cheek,
and we share the love and joy
that comes from you.

For when I see a bird

Dear God who pays attention to the birds,
There are some birds outside my window.
They fly back and forth between the trees.
There are so many sizes and shapes and colors.
You notice each one!
Thank you for the birds.

For meal time

Dear God who makes good things,
You lovingly feed your creation.
For the farmer who raised the food,
for the gardener who planted the seed,
for the honeybee that helped it grow,
for the workers who gathered the crop,
and for the hands that prepared this food,
we thank you.

For when I have to eat something I don't like

God, I'd rather be eating something else.

Help me to still be grateful.

Thank you for the way this food makes my body strong.

I wonder if you ever had to eat something you didn't like.

Let my "eating it anyway" give you praise.

For taking a bath

God, I love to feel the warm water on my skin.
I love to splash and make bubble beards!
I want to stay in until my toes are wrinkled
and then wrap up in a fluffy towel,
warm and clean and smelling sweet.
Help me take care of this good body.
You know and love each part!

For brushing my teeth

God, I brush my teeth every day
because my mouth is really important!
(Sometimes I need reminding.)
I use it to eat, laugh, and share feelings and stories.
My smile can brighten someone's day.
My kind words can heal someone's hurt.
Help me take care of this marvelous mouth,
because I will sing to you forever
with my lips, gums, and teeth!

For an everyday day

Today was just an everyday day.
Kind of in the middle.
But ordinary days have
good things in them:
a place to sleep,
people who love me,
things to eat and drink,
stories to tell.
And you are always with me.

For a hard day

This was not my favorite day, God.
If I were putting my days in order
from super-favorite to completely awful,
this one was pretty bad.
Thank you that I don't have to pretend that things are okay.
You can bring good even from terrible days.
Help me to trust you when all I can see is what's hard.

For a really great day

I dream about days like today.
Days where
everything I hope for happens.
Days where
everyone gets along.
Days where
even work is fun.
These days give me a little peek
into heaven:
when everything will be right,
when my heart will always say,
"This is the best day ever."
Thank you, God.

For when I look at the stars

There are so many stars filling up your sky,
and there are millions I can't even see.
Wow!
In the Bible, you said you would
make a family like the stars—
so many people we couldn't even count them if we tried!
You look at us like we look at the stars—
shining and breathtaking and beloved.

For bedtime

Dear Maker of the stars and the moon that shine in the night,
Thank you for another day.
Thank you for every moment when my heart was glad.

I ask for comfort for every moment that made me sad.
Forgive me for the times I didn't follow your best way.
Be near to me as I sleep.

A note from the authors

As people made in God's image, all of us—including children—are worthy of robust spiritual formation. Prayer is an important element of spiritual formation, but our prayers do not need to be long or complicated. That is why this collection of simple prayers is intended to help us connect with God in the ordinary moments of every day.

It's in these daily moments—around the dinner table, on the way to visit a friend, when pointing out a bird in the tree—that we learn to recognize God's closeness and God's kingdom in the world. This is how our hearts and minds are formed and shaped by the gospel.

We want this book to support you—the guides and shepherds who come alongside children. We hope that you will not only share this book at home, but that it will also travel along with you—in the car, in your bag, or on errands. And as you practice praying these small prayers together in your comings and goings, we also hope you start noticing other moments when you or the children you are with want to talk to God.

Here are a few things you could talk and think about as you read together:

- Do you ever think about God being with you when you . . . [brush your teeth, play outside, or something else]?

- How does that make you feel?

- What parts of your day would you write a prayer for?

Above all, we hope the habit of talking with God shapes children as they grow, and that they always know that God desires to come close to them.